you're a Nice Guy, But you're Bad in Bed

A simple, unapologetic guide to help you behave like a decent human being in the bedroom.

Elsie Gilmore

SECOND EDITION

Inside illustrations by Craig Shorey | https://craigshorey.com/

Elsie Gilmore | https://elsiegilmore.com

contents

Dedication

Dedicated to men who are willing to listen and learn.

♥

Intro

Hello! We might have sex! Clearly, there is something about you that is sweet, warm, and nice. We've probably hung out and had a great time talking and laughing. Maybe we went dancing or had a nice meal. And now there's a chance we'll take it to the next level.

You're probably adorably dorky and not traditionally good-looking. Or maybe you're a total hunk with a nerdy edge. Either way, it looks like we may rub our naughty bits together.

Because I think you're a nice guy, I want to tell you in the most loving and respectful way that you may be bad in bed. This booklet outlines different ways men can be good sexual partners, and you may recognize that some or all of them are things you normally don't do or think about.

On a basic level, being good in bed is not about techniques, experience, or positions. It's about **listening**, **paying attention**, and **being considerate**.

This booklet is to help you be a better lover. As a nice guy, I hope you will take to heart some of the wisdom I am about to impart. **Even a one-night stand can be enjoyable if you go into it with the right attitude and knowledge.**

The Approach

Let's start from the beginning

Before you even think about having sex with me or any other woman, let's talk about how you ended up in bed with a woman to begin with. Because if you start off on the wrong foot, it's hard to have a good experience.

I'm sure you've heard of a little thing called "consent." It means that before you have sex with a woman, you should make sure she honestly wants to have sex with you. Did you know that having sex with a very intoxicated woman means you didn't get consent? Why? Because a drunk woman cannot give consent. She is not of sound mind to say yes or no to sex. "She didn't say no" is not a legitimate argument that she wanted to have sex with you or that consent was given. You might think, "But I was drunk also."

That really doesn't matter. You should never, ever have sex with someone who is extremely inebriated, even if you're in a relationship with them. One of you could get injured or forget to use protection. It's a recipe for bad things to happen.

Another way that men sometimes get coerced or passive "consent" is by badgering a woman to have sex with them. Or by starting to have sex with a woman who is protesting and then thinking it's OK to continue if she stops protesting. It is possible she has just decided that you will not listen to her anymore and is letting you have sex with her out of frustration. That is NOT OK, and you're basically assaulting her at that point. If you ever feel like you are having sex TO a woman instead of WITH a woman, you probably do not have consent. Pestering a woman into having sex with you when she is telling you no or resisting is NOT OK. Please do not ever have sex with a woman who you have to "convince." You should only have sex with people who clearly and vocally want to have sex and want to have it with you at that moment. You should never make assumptions about what a woman wants. You should get clear and explicit confirmation that she is eager and willing to have sex.

Just because a woman goes home with you does not mean she wants to have sex with you. And, even if she does initially want to have sex with you, there are a million reasons why she might change her mind. Maybe she starts getting a different vibe from you. Maybe something you do in the meantime makes her feel differently than she did a few minutes or an hour ago. It doesn't really matter. Once she has changed her mind, please respect that. I know you think it's not fair, but it IS fair, and it is NOT OK to continue if she is no longer into it. You can ask her why she changed her mind, but the important thing to remember is that if you continue, you are now having sex with someone who doesn't want to have sex with you. The best thing to do is to leave her alone and try to talk about it later.

Similarly, if the terms of the sex change during sex, and she does not agree to those terms, you should stop immediately. For example, if you start having a kind of sex she did not agree to and does not want to have. Also, if a condom breaks, you should stop having sex immediately to get a new one. Lots of things can happen during sex that might kill the mood for either person, and you should respect that.

Things to Know

Let's go over some things you should understand about women

If you think you know everything about women, you probably don't! Always be open to learning about the science of female sexuality and individual women's nuances. If you love sex, you should be willing to learn new things about it throughout your life. While most women will have similarities, they aren't a one-size-fits-all deal. Here are some things to keep in mind.

1. **Women like sex.** Many women really enjoy sex, just like men. Most women like to orgasm and experience pleasure. They get horny and want to fuck, just like you.

2. **Only 25% of women can orgasm via penetration alone.** While some women can orgasm through penetration alone, 70% need manual or oral stimulation to orgasm.[1] Only 5% of women are unable to orgasm, and some people argue that the g-spot doesn't exist[2].

3. **Most women don't want quick sex.** Women's "engine" usually needs time to heat up, and that means foreplay (which, you know, can actually be quite enjoyable). Think of it this way: men are like flamethrowers, and women are like ovens. Besides, no one wants to feel rushed. **Sex is supposed to be fun and relaxing.** If you're not making enough time for sex, make more. (And no, sex doesn't have to be hours of sweaty pleasure every time, but a quickie doesn't always cut it.)

4. **Women often work hard to make sexual experiences good for men.** Women often say and do things for your benefit because we want sex to be mutually enjoyable. We try to make the experience good for you, and we'd like you to do the same for us because we like you and enjoy your company.

Things to Do

Things men can do to be good sexual partners

FOR STARTERS, HAVE SEX WITH PEOPLE YOU LIKE.
This may seem like common sense, but being a good lover works best when you have some sort of

admiration or affection for the person you're having sex with. Even if it's a one-night stand. If you like the person, you're more likely to treat them with respect in bed.

In 2015, Dr. John Gottman, of the Gottman Institute – an organization that pursues a research-based approach to relationships - gave a presentation in front of the National Rotary during which he relayed that a man once asked him if there would ever be a Viagra for women that made them more amorous and want to have sex more often. Dr. Gottman said, "You know they've already invented that." And the man excitedly asked, "Where can I get that?" Dr. Gottman replied, "Well, it's called listening."[1]

GET HER ENGINE HEATED UP. Any time you spend on foreplay is time for the woman to produce natural wetness in her vagina that will come in handy during sex. You can start with kissing and move on to touching. Pay attention to her reactions when you touch her. Make sure she's on board. Make it playful.

FIND OUT WHAT GIVES HER AN ORGASM. I assume if you're having sex with someone you like that you want her to experience pleasure and an orgasm, if possible. Giving a woman an orgasm is not always what you think. **In general, clitoral stimulation (oral**

or manual) will give her an orgasm, but there are nuances to what makes each woman orgasm.

Don't assume that just having vaginal sex with her is going to magically cause her to orgasm or that simply by having sex with her, you've tried to give her an orgasm. You haven't. Ask her to give herself an orgasm so you can watch and learn, or ask her what works best. You should not assume that what your last partner liked is what your current sexual partner will like or that your current sexual partner can orgasm like your previous one did. You can definitely try things, but if they don't work, don't be afraid to ask questions.

You may already know that you are likely going to orgasm, but this is a team sport. I shouldn't have to tell you that women want to orgasm, too. **Women will often go to great lengths to help you orgasm, and you should return the favor.**

If you have trouble coming to orgasm during sex, that is an excellent opportunity for you to model good communication for your partner. If you can't orgasm, you can still show her what makes you feel good. And if you can, you can show her the tricks.

ERR ON THE SIDE OF BEING TOO GENTLE. Like your naughty bits, her naughty bits are very delicate.

You can rub them vigorously without using too much pressure to make sure no damage is done. Being too rough can result in chafing, bruising, and soreness later. Let her remember how good you made her feel, not how abrasive you were to her nether regions. It is better to start out gently and ask if that works for her. I'll be honest: she might lie. Because women often feel uncomfortable speaking up or don't want to be seen as complaining, pay attention to her body language to ensure that you're not hurting her. Is she grimacing? Is she flinching? Or is she making yummy noises and moving her hips toward you?

As you can see, women will often have had terrible experiences with men before you. You should assume this, and you should try not to be another one of them. Women need a kind sexual partner to help them heal from previous damage. You can be that person for her if you're patient and care about her.

ALWAYS LET HER KNOW THAT HER ORGASM IS IMPORTANT, TOO. The woman's orgasm is as important as yours. If you make it a rule to be sure she has an orgasm first, you can feel good every time, knowing that you're a thoughtful person. Plus, she will look at you with googly eyes. Women have been "taught," through repeated examples, that their orgasm isn't important. Many men want to rush through it, half-ass it, or ignore it altogether. Because of this, she might have a mental block about cumming. It will help if you are not in a hurry. You can reassure her that you're not in a hurry. **If she can't cum, don't immediately stop paying attention to her pleasure.** You can still touch, kiss, caress her, and tell her you can't wait to try again. **Giving a woman an orgasm is immensely satisfying and qualifies you for a gold star every time. You should give it your full attention.**

DO NOT FORCE HER TO DO ANYTHING. This may sound obvious, but it happens more than you'd imagine. And you may have done it without thinking about it. It includes things like pushing her head down onto or further onto your penis. This move is violent, unbelievably rude, and demanding. Use your words to encourage her instead. She will do what she's comfortable with. If she's not comfortable with it, you shouldn't try to make her do it. Say things like, "Would you like to do this?" "I'd like to do this now. Is that OK?" "What would you like to do?" "Can we try this?" "I would like it if you did this. Are you OK with that?" Communication should be a massive part of any sexual experience, especially with someone new.

This is especially true when it comes to things like choking. I have had guys tell me they will "try" this on women without prior permission. Do not ever, ever, ever put your hand on a woman's throat without discussing it beforehand. And this is never something to do on a first sexual encounter unless you have extensively discussed it beforehand, set limits, and established safe words or gestures. Please try not to traumatize or further traumatize women during sex. One in four women has been sexually assaulted, and this kind of move can feel like another assault.

The same goes for spanking unless you're intending to spank only very lightly. It's best to discuss these things outside the bedroom first because she may be reluctant to speak up once you're there.

LISTEN. Do not ask a woman a question in bed, ignore her answer, and then give her two choices she didn't express interest in. If you want her to do something, ask specifically. "Do you want to do _____?" If she says "Yes," then great. If she says no, move on to something different. Also, if she says "Stop," "Slow down," or "Let's change position," then do those things. Don't ignore her. She may be experiencing discomfort or pain. Sex must be consensual at all times, or, well, it is no longer sex.

Part of listening is creating a safe space where your partner knows she will be heard. If you constantly ask for her input and then ignore it, she will not feel comfortable being honest with you in the future, and she will likely stop having sex with you.

ALWAYS USE LUBE WHEN NECESSARY. This should be common sense. It really hurts when you try to push your penis or even finger into a dry vagina or anus. Wet it with something! You can either use your saliva or (better) some lube. Why would you want to cause pain? Wetter is better. You may want her to stick something inside you sometime, and then you'll know what I mean.

ALWAYS WEAR A CONDOM UNLESS THERE IS AN AGREEMENT NOT TO. Don't want to use a condom? Why aren't you concerned about diseases? What if she gets pregnant? How do you know if she's on the pill? Always ask if the woman wants you to wear a condom before you get too far along. If she does, do NOT try to have sex with her without one on. It's dangerous and disrespectful. It's also a crime.

HAVE FUN. Sex should be about the journey, not just the destination. Enjoy the woman's body. Appreciate her quirks and features. Play, have fun, laugh, talk. Make it an experience worth remembering. Don't get so wrapped up in reaching orgasm that you jackhammer the woman for 10 or 15 minutes in a frenzy. That's not enjoyable. If you are having trouble cumming, take a break. Do some touching. She will likely think less of you for the jackhammering than because you couldn't reach orgasm. **Most women aren't judging your performance in bed.** They just want you to treat them respectfully and pay attention to their needs.

COMMUNICATE. Is there something you need? Shout it out. Don't get frustrated. Women are generally patient and understanding in bed. **Talk about what you need.** If you want to do something kinky, discuss it first. She wants this to be a mutually pleasurable experience and to know that you are present with her. My advice, though, is to get good at having plain old regular sex together first. Not everyone wants to get kinky, and those who do usually want to build trust with the other person first.

BE GENEROUS. If you're just looking for somewhere to ejaculate, please use your hand. Women are not sperm receptacles, and we don't like to be treated like an afterthought during sex. **Take pride in making sure your partner has an orgasm.** Make it your mission. Otherwise, what will her impression be of having sex with you? Will she want to have sex with you again? Use some forethought. Think about how much you like her as a person. She's probably having sex with you because she likes you, too.

BE HUMBLE. Treat sex with reverence, even a one-night stand. Be open to learning and growing. Women often have to overcome various fears when they choose to have sex. They have likely had much different sexual experiences than you have.

AFTERWARDS. Many women like to continue to feel intimate after the act. Don't jump up, rush to the shower, and/or leave in a hurry. Linger in the afterglow. Don't make assumptions about what will happen next. Perhaps ask, after 10-15 minutes of quiet snuggling during which you deeply appreciate that this woman has shared her body with you, "Should I go?" Try to find out specifically what she wants. If she's at your place, "Would you like to stay over? We could grab breakfast." or "I really need to get to sleep but would love to see you again." Make sure she's OK to drive. Walk her to her car if it's dark out. Communicating about what comes next can avoid unnecessary awkwardness.

Special Notes

Special notes for the well-endowed

If you were endowed with a large penis and think this automatically makes you good in bed, I have some bad news: bigger is not always better. First, many women will not be able to take your large penis inside their mouth or vagina. Second, there is more to sex than penis size, and women who can't orgasm vaginally will still not be able to, regardless of the size of your penis. So, get that tongue limbered up.

Beyond that, here are a few rules to keep in mind:

Be extra gentle and considerate. If she says, "It's too deep." Do not respond with, "How can it be TOO deep?" That question is insensitive, ignorant, and mean. If you don't think it can be too deep, try buying a dildo the size of your penis and sticking the entire length of it up your own ass. Large penises can be difficult to suck as well. Please be responsible with your large penis. You can legitimately hurt people with it.

Read people's limits. You should never expect or coerce anyone into having anal sex, especially if you have a large penis. See my advice for the previous item. If she says "no" or acts reluctant, let it go. You can cause irritation and lasting pain, even if you're careful. You should never inflict unwanted pain just so you can have pleasure.

Conclusion

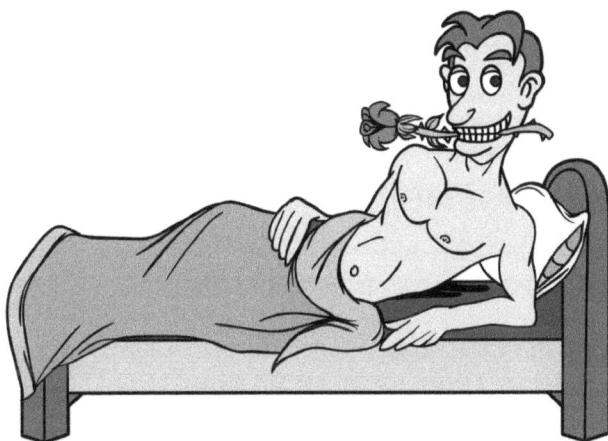

Time to apply what you've learned

I'm sure you need some time to digest this information and figure out how to put it into practice. Some men don't think they can control their manly urges in bed, so they make excuses for the way they act during sex. That's bullshit. All you need to do is truly look at and acknowledge the nice woman having sex with you. See her as a human being and your equal – someone who likes you and wants both of you to experience pleasure. You may think, "But I've never had any complaints before." Women often try to protect men's feelings. Just because you haven't had complaints doesn't mean women haven't found something you've done in bed to be unpleasant. Women often trade sex for companionship and put up with bad behavior as part of that trade.

Because you are a nice person, women may want to have sex with you. But your negative sexual behaviors may confuse them and push them away. Sex should be a conversation, even (and especially) when it's with someone you don't know well. You should be learning things about her, not making assumptions or ignoring her needs altogether.

Please try to be attentive and considerate in bed so women can have more, better sex with you.

About the Author

Elsie Gilmore began her writing journey when the internet was a mere toddler and hasn't stopped since. Her work includes various personal and professional blogs, a column for the Rutland Herald, participation in several radio shows, and her current weekly Substack publication, Sunday Mornings in Bed. Described as "that lady who will not stop talking," Elsie's voice is both persistent and passionate.

With a career spanning twenty years as a web developer and the founder of Women With Moxie, a women's networking company, Elsie has worn many hats. From Vermont farm girl to multi-business owner to published author, she continues to pursue the awesome sauce in life. Stay tuned for her upcoming guide: *How to Find Joy in a Capitalist Hellscape* (October 2024).

To find more creative work by Elsie Gilmore, visit https://elsiegilmore.com

You can find Elsie Gilmore on Amazon at

https://www.amazon.com/stores/Elsie-Gilmore/author/B08SL7VHTL

Love this booklet? Drop a review on Amazon.

https://www.amazon.com/Youre-Nice-Guy-But-Bad-ebook/dp/B08SKS1N8R/

Endnotes

Things to Know

1. Castleman, Michael. "The Most Important Sexual Statistic." *Psychology Today*, 16 March 2009, www.psychologytoday.com/us/blog/all-about-sex/200903/the-most-important-sexual-statistic. Accessed 25 June 2024.

2. Jaslow, Ryan. "Does a Woman's G-Spot Actually Exist? Study Has Answer." *CBS News*, 5 Jan. 2012, www.cbsnews.com/news/does-a-womans-g-spot-actually-exist-study-has-answer/. Accessed 25 June 2024.

Things to Do

1. Gottman, John. "Making Relationships Work." *Seattle Rotary Club*, 2015, YouTube, www.youtube.com/watch?v=8YpnDao8TQs. Accessed 25 June 2024.

www.ingramcontent.com/pod-product-compliance
Lightning Source LLC
Chambersburg PA
CBHW052026030426
42335CB00026B/3306